The Needs of Billy
And Other Autistic Children

Dawn Adams

AuthorHouse™
1663 Liberty Drive
Bloomington, IN 47403
www.authorhouse.com
Phone: 1-800-839-8640

Published by AuthorHouse 03/03/2015

ISBN: 978-1-4969-4777-2 (sc)
ISBN: 978-1-4969-7058-9 (hc)
ISBN: 978-1-4969-4778-9 (e)

Library of Congress Control Number: 2014918984

Print information available on the last page.

This book is printed on acid-free paper.

authorHOUSE®

Contents

Our Son Billy

When our son Billy was diagnosed as being autistic, we knew little of this wide spread, and increasing, condition. Since then, through intensive research, going to meetings and speaking with hundreds of others, we realize the devastation and heart break of this horrific condition.

I brought Billy to school on his very first day. He was soon to be 4 years old. Billy was hesitant at first, but as he was getting into the classroom he was really enjoying being around the other children. During the first few months of school, I would hide in his classroom from time to time to see how he was really doing.

Every morning, I would start my routine with Billy. I'd wake him up, get him dressed for school, cook his breakfast, brush his hair and his teeth, wash his hands and face, put on his backpack, and then Billy would always stand in front of the picture window and wait for the school bus to come up the street. He'd be so excited when the bus came to the house. He would throw his arms up and down in excitement and have the biggest smile on his face. And then I would walk him to the school bus, kiss him, and wait for the bus to leave. Mostly out of sight.

And every day when Billy came home from school, I would always have a snack ready for him. While he was eating, I would read everything the teachers sent home in the book bag. For the first few years, the teachers would send home a progress report for that day. How your child did that day. What he or she responded to and what they didn't; then I would spend more time with him in that particular area. In each class there would be one teacher and at least one teacher's aide. I would also continue with whatever else they were teaching that day.

However, we all started to notice that the following day reports were on subjects totally different from the day before. They were teaching these classes like a regular class room instead of a special needs class.

Most special needs children cannot comprehend anything as fast as a child in a regular class room. I realize that they have to move on, but really as soon as the next day! From what we have experienced from talking with several other people from different areas, a lot of the teachers aren't really qualified to teach special needs. I don't think they're bad teachers, just not special needs teachers. And some teachers do not have the patience needed to teach them.

A lot of special needs children need one on one. That's why there's a teacher aide in the classroom. Also special needs children have very limited attention spans. Getting a child to stay interested for 10 to 15 minutes at a time is great when you are teaching them. I would be a great special needs teachers. I have the patience, which is very important. I would still go over and over and over the same thing until I feel that he has grasped the concept.

I realize that teachers don't have that much time, but from what I have seen, they could spend a lot more time than they do. That's one area where the teacher's aide is supposed to help. Most classes have between 9 - 12 children, one teaching aide. Some of the aide's Billy has had, would just sit there next to him, playing with him mostly.

I also feel some of the special needs children are different when it comes to their learning abilities. They may have a class filled with just autistic children.

Even though they are the same age, and have the same disability that doesn't mean they can learn something as fast as another child. Every year Billy gets tested to see what learning age he's at, at that time. Unfortunately, Billy's been a few years behind. We learned that he doesn't mentally grow a year every year. In his case we were told he would mentally age hopefully around six months every year.

When Billy was in the first grade, we noticed the children in his class were being taught as if they were 5 and 6 year olds, when mentally they were only 3 and 4 years old. The teachers would go on as they would for a normal first grade class. One example I witnessed, the teacher was telling her class to draw a picture of their favorite toy. Really, was I hearing this correctly? I prayed not. But unfortunately I did hear correctly. There were 9 children in the class that day. And out of the nine only two children could talk. All but one of the children was scribbling on the paper. The other child just sat there. None of the children in Billy's class were being assisted. The teacher would lay the paper and crayons down in front of them and go and attend to something else.

Every parent or grandparent I spoke with over the years, tell me the same thing when their child starts school. When they meet the teacher for the first time they tell them in detail, about the medical problems their child has and that they need to be aware of. The teacher writes this in their chart. Then from time to time the parents send notes and letters or even calls to the teacher reminding them of their child's needs when they notice something wasn't done.

Unfortunately in Billy's case, he was progressing slowly. So even though the school system is moving him up every year, we still go over everything until he catches on and understands.

The school systems in our country are getting worse instead of better. State agencies aren't funding for special needs children like they once were. Billy doesn't come home with any type of reports anymore. Unless we call the teachers, or go sit in their classroom we don't know what's being taught right then.

That's when I started going to meetings, and going around to different schools in different states to see what they were teaching. How they were teaching and what products they were using to teach during the year. So we could go and buy products very similar.

How about the children who cannot talk? Most of the children with autism can't talk. Not one public school that I visited was teaching sign language or any other form of communicating back and forth. Not one. However in some of the private schools they do. However, most parents cannot afford to send their child to private schools.

I know they have programs on the computers now for special needs. And I think that's really great. But most of the young special needs children could care less about computers.

Why would you start teaching them on a computer when they are trying to learn in a different way since they started school. We bought him a notebook when he 12 or 13 years old I believe. He could care less. The more we tried the less interested he was. I'm not sure if the high functioning special needs child react the same way or not. I never witnessed a computer in the class room.

Most parents now have to buy school supplies several times a year now for their special needs children, because most of the schools no longer supply the necessary supplies that's needed. And if they do, it's not enough. I've seen teachers that want her class to do a project, asking the parents to help out buying some supplies. Buying learning supplies all the time gets expensive. Everything is sold separately. And it always seems that half get lost or thrown out by mistake. This is one reason I started doing this book.

Choosing some of the best toys.

When buying toys for learning, we would choose toys that will help your child's developmental needs. Also to keep the child interested as long as possible. Make playtime fun and educational.

Play with your child board games that will keep their interest. Take them outside as often as you can and play ball. Have him/her to catch the ball as often as possible.

Most children love dress up, it's just at different ages younger the better. A good time to start is around Halloween. Especially as it's a great time to see when they begin to get excited dressing up, and then go out trick or treating.

Also play pretend roles with your children. Little boys like playing pretend just as much as little girls. Little girls like pretending to be mommies, so make sure you have little dolls, doll houses, dolls clothing, little strollers, etc, for your little girl. If he/she wants to pretend to be a baker, try to buy them an easy bake oven, little pots and pans for children, and plastic condiments so they can play the role. (If you use an easy bake oven, make sure you or someone else in the house can be there with them because they are electric and get very warm.)

If your child wants to be a police man or a police woman or a fireman get the outfits and amenities they will need to carry out their roles, and so on.

Children also love stuffed animals. For the children who cannot talk, buy the stuffed animals that will help them imitate the sounds of words.

One way to improve their skills is to play with toys that draw their attention to who is speaking. This is what you want, to get and keep their attention. Pass the animal back and forth so they will know who is in control right then.

We have found it very important to a special needs child to praise them a lot after they learn something for the first time. We'd tell him over and over how proud we are of him. Then we would clap and say "great going Billy." And we would do it for at least 30 seconds. And Billy would always show how happy he was. He would giggle and swing his arms up and down and do his little dance. Of course mom would always kiss on him for about a minute. Billy rarely pulled away when I would continue to kiss on him. I was so happy he didn't mind when I would do that.

When he was learning how to write, we would hold our hand over his and draw the same letter over and over and over until he could do it by his self. This requires a lot of patience. I do mean a lot of patience. When you start teaching them sign language, don't be upset if this takes months if not years. Always keep in mind their attention span is very limited. But when they learn they usually always remember.

When Billy doesn't want to do anything that he always knows how to do, he'll pretend not knowing how to do it. That's when you have to be stern. Of course mom would let him get away with it, but not very often. I always had to remind myself it's really for his own good.

At Christmas time when all the presents were under the tree, Billy never went near them. He was only excited over the tree, lights and ornaments. When it was time to open the presents, he still never reacted with excitement. Only when he saw that it was a toy or stuffed animal did he react with excitement. The more sounds it made or the more colors he saw, the louder with excitement he showed. Just like with other children. When he saw clothes or books, no reaction, but when he saw that it was a toy he was very excited.

My time going from school to school.

During the past 13 years I would go to other schools and watch how the children would act when the teachers gave them play time. They would grab any toy on the shelf and try to figure out what it was, or they would either sit there or stand there in the play area. In some schools this would on from 20 - 35 minutes. Then it was time to eat lunch and take a nap. All together the time spent doing nothing was between 90 - 115 minutes. When they woke up, it was time to watch a movie. Another 30-45 minutes. After the movie, the teacher and the teacher's aides would get the children ready to go home.

Half of the day was wasted. Don't get me wrong, I realize doing all this is necessary but not back to back. Too much time is wasted. Why not do a 30 minute movie one day and have play time the following day.

Of course the teacher's and the aides can't get them interested any more for the rest of the day. They're too relaxed.

The classes aren't as long as they for the regular school classes. And I believe that all the children's classes shouldn't be wasted for that long each day.

Something else I noticed frequently. The children who are not potty trained. When the teacher feels like it's time for them to use the bathroom, they put the child on the toilet and leave them there for at least 15 minutes. I have also witnessed to this more times that I ever wanted to. Can you imagine leaving them there for 15 minutes or longer and then to find out they have already gone in their pants. I guess checking their pants first would make more sense. Billy came home several times with rings on his bottom.

I do want add first that parents who aren't raising their children has no say so when they have an opinion on how the teacher or the aides are teaching their classes. However, most of the time they said they would look into it, but rarely was something done.

At times like these is when the family has to work harder to make up for the time lost.

It's very hard when both parents have to go and work to make ends meet.

But I always looked into every program available for Billy. Even if it took months for him to be able to benefit from these programs, I would stay on it.

I would go back for the next two days to see if this was a daily routine and it was.

Mikey's Big Adventure

Mikey had always wanted to go on a long adventure. For a long time he always knew where he wanted to go and what he wanted to do. And he wanted to go on this big adventure alone so he could see the things he wanted to see and do the things he wanted to do and stay as long as he wanted.

For days Mikey was packing for his adventure and checking his list over and over again to make sure he wouldn't forget anything. Mikey wanted to camp out some nights so he could see all the stars in the sky, and realized he needed a telescope to do that.

The first day Mikey thought he would go to his grandpa and grandma's house to borrow their telescope. The first night of Mikey's adventure he camped out in the beautiful mountains of North Carolina. Mikey thought, 'there aren't any pretty mountains in Connecticut like there are in North Carolina'.

As Mikey was setting up his tent and unpacking what he needed for the night, he would lie there and look up at the sky and try to count all the stars. And while he was counting he heard a small noise. So he put down the telescope and took out his flashlight and started looking around the camp site. The noise was getting louder and louder. Mikey thought to himself it sounds like a baby animal.

Later as Mikey was getting closer to the mountains he came upon a small den. And inside the den was a small puppy, all by himself. Mikey kept looking and looking for the puppy's dad and mom but they weren't there. So Mikey picked up the puppy and carried him back to his tent. The puppy was really hungry and thirsty. After Mikey laid the puppy down on his blanket, he started fixing the puppy something to eat and drink. When he was finished the puppy walked over to Mikey's pillow and fell asleep. He fed the puppy every day.

When Mikey was really to leave the camp site, he folded up his tent and packed everything up, and was telling the puppy good-bye. But the puppy had other plans. He wanted to hang around Mikey. Every time Mikey tried to leave, the puppy would follow. Finally Mickey told the puppy he could come with him. The puppy was so small Mikey put him in his shirt pocket.

Mikey said to the puppy, "I have to give you a name. What name can I give you that we both like?" How about Duke? 'Do you like that name?' Mikey asked. I like that name too. Every day Mickey would tell Duke where they were going next. Mikey was starting to love Duke very much and was very happy that they were going on this adventure together.

Today Mikey was planning to see a museum about cowboys. "How would you like to see cowboys today Duke?" Mikey asked. It will be a lot of fun. Your name is after an old cowboy name Duke. Everyday Mikey would tell Duke how much he loved him.

The museum was great but he couldn't stay long because of Duke. The lady wanted him to keep Duke outside. And he couldn't do that so they left.

The next day, he and Duke visited his other grandpa and grandma in Georgia. His grandma is scared of dogs, but because Duke was so small she said he could come in the house. Grandpa and grandma fell in love with little Duke.

After dinner, they all went for a walk around the neighborhood. All the other kids loved Duke.

The next morning Grandpa and I went swimming in the pool. Grandma was holding little Duke. Little Duke didn't want to get in the pool at all. Grandma said little Duke really loves me. And Mikey said I love him too. He's my best friend.

After lunch, Grandma took Mikey shopping and little Duke stayed home with Grandpa. Grandma bought Mikey some new clothes and she bought little Duke his own bedding. Grandma bought him a small pillow with a pillow case and blanket that had Sponge Bob on them and a stuffed animal.

That night Grandpa, Grandma, Duke and Mikey were watching a football game. Giants against the Patriots. Grandpa and Grandma wanted the Patriots to win and Duke and Mikey wanted the Giants to win. Duke and Mikey were very happy because their team won.

The next day they all wanted to see the new museum that had been built close to their house. Mikey was so excited because this one was about the Indians. He couldn't wait to get there. He always watched cowboy and Indian movies on television and now he got to see how they really dressed and lived, and the food they grew and ate.

It was a lot of fun. Tomorrow would be the last day of his big adventure. He and little Duke had a lot of fun. And now it was time to go back home to see his family. He really missed everyone. And he couldn't wait for them to meet little Duke.

Chelsea and Sam at the beach

My name is Chelsea and my dog's name is Sam. Last year when I turned four years old, we moved into a new house with a swimming pool. I was scared of the water, but Sam wanted to jump right in. He wanted to swim every day.

Dad and Mom thought it was time that too learned how to swim. So when the weather started to get warmer, Mom started to teach me how to swim almost every day, so I wouldn't be scared and they wouldn't worry all the time about me drowning.

Every time I was in the pool, Sam would jump in too. Sam already knew how to swim. Mom said, "Most animals know how to swim from the day they were born". After a few weeks I was swimming with Sam all by myself. I couldn't dive off the diving board yet by myself but Dad said he would teach me.

When Daddy came home from work he said, "Chelsea, I have a big surprise for you and Sam." I said,"what is it Daddy, what is it? What is the big surprise? Daddy said, "How would you and Sam like to go to the beach when school is out with Mommy and me"? asked "What is the beach Daddy"? Daddy said, "The beach is like a really big swimming pool. And around the water is a lot of sand, like you play with in a sand box". I said, "WOW".

"Can I bring some toys too?" Daddy said, "sure you can Chelsea."

Today was the last day of school. When the school bell rang, all the kids jumped up from their desks and ran outside. When I got to the door, Mom and Sam were waiting to walk me home. We are so happy because Dad said when school was out we all are going to the beach.

That night Dad came home and said, "who wants to go to the beach tomorrow with Mom and me"? And I said, "we do." The next morning after breakfast, Dad, Mom, Sam and I started to get everything we would need to spend the day at the beach. Sam and I would see the beach for the first time.

Mom said, "Chelsea and Sam look, there's the beach." I said, "WOW, look at all the water." After we laid everything down on our blanket, Dad took my hand and we were walking towards all that water. It looked like all the water in the world to me.

Sam was so excited he was running real fast to jump into the water. Dad called for Sam to slow down, but he kept running. When Sam got to the water he was hopping up and down, then back to us and back to the water. Sam was so happy.

When Dad and I put our feet into the water, it was a lot different from our swimming pool. Dad again reached for my hand and said, "It's okay Chelsea, just hold my hand and stay real close".

"Sam, Sam come back", Dad yelled. Sam was going out further and further into the water and we were really getting worried.

I was scared because Sam wasn't listening to Dad. And Sam was my best friend in the whole world. Dad called for Mom to come stand near me so he could go out into the water to get Sam. Mom and I just stood there watching Dad swim faster and faster. As Dad got near Sam, Sam was really tired and couldn't swim anymore. Dad got to him just in time. As Dad was swimming back to us, he was carrying Sam. When they were getting out of the water, Sam was really tired. He kept licking us all over our faces.

Mom went back to our blanket and started preparing our lunch.Sam was really hungry from all the swimming, and when he finished eating he had a long nap. Mom, Dad and I were watching the other kids swim and play on the sand.

This was the best day ever.

Teaching at home

It was much easier for me to learn sign language before teaching someone else. I was constantly looking back and forth. Also in our experience not going over and over and over the same thing before they understand what you are teaching them they easily forget.

Special needs children have a very short attention span. From all the children I have witnessed over the years, when they are being taught on a one on one basis, the teachers or aides would teach for about 15 minutes and then let the child rest for about 5 minutes, and so on and so on.

The charts and illustrations in this book were being taught in all the schools that I visited.

All children try to distract you and keep you from continuing on. Billy knew exactly how to get me to stop teaching him and just play. He would smile so cute from ear to ear, or just start laughing for no reason, and it worked for a few moments, then I had to show him it's not time to play.

We still give him a snack when he would get home from school. Giving him a small snack first then play with him for about 10 - 15 minutes before we sat him down to begin teaching him was very beneficial.

Some Of The Mouth Toys We Used for

Oral Motor Skills

- Tape Recorders

- Bubbles

- Wind Instruments (musical)

- Whistles

Help Improve Hand Strength

- Dough

- Clay

Art Toys For Fine Motor Skills

- Colored Pencils

- Colored Paper/Plain Paper

- Crayons

- Markers

- Paintbrushes

- Paint

Indoor Toys For Motor Skills

- Large Balls - For Hopping

- Tents

- Tunnels

Choosing some of the best toys.

When buying Billy toys for learning, we would choose toys that will help your child's developmental needs. Also to keep the child interested as long as possible. Make playtime fun and educational.

Play with your child board games that will keep their interest. Take them outside as often as you can and play ball. Have him/her to catch the ball as often as possible.

Most children love dress up, it's just at different ages younger the better. A good time to start is around Halloween. Especially as it's a great time to see when they begin to get excited dressing up, and then go out trick or treating.

Also play pretend roles with your children. Little boys like playing pretend just as much as little girls. Little girls like pretending to be mommies, so make sure you have little dolls, doll houses, dolls clothing, little strollers, etc, for your little girl. If he/she wants to pretend to be a baker, try to buy them an easy bake oven, little pots and pans for children, and plastic condiments so they can play the role. (If you use an easy bake oven, make sure you or someone else in the house can be there with them because they are electric and get very warm.)

If your child wants to be a police man or a police woman or a fireman get the outfits and amenities they will need to carry out their roles, and soon.

Which one is the Sun, Moon and Star?

Which one is the Grasshopper ?

Which one is the zebra ?

Which is the

Seal ?

Octopus ?

Which one is the

Dump-Pick Up truck ?

Which one is the leave ?

What color is the banana ?

What color is the pumpkin?

What do you put on

your feet ?

Which one can you play with at the beach?

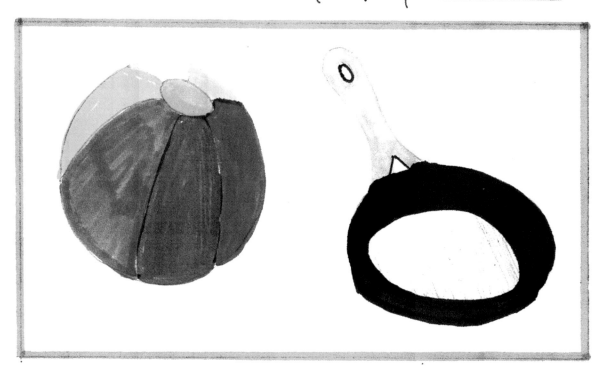

What do babies drink out of?

Which one do you eat at Thanksgiving?

Which one do you open up?

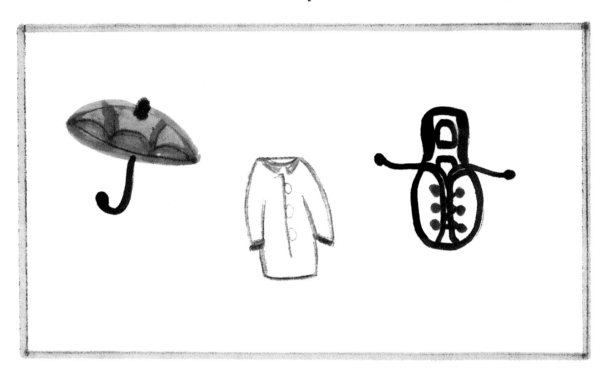

Which one do you use for coloring books?

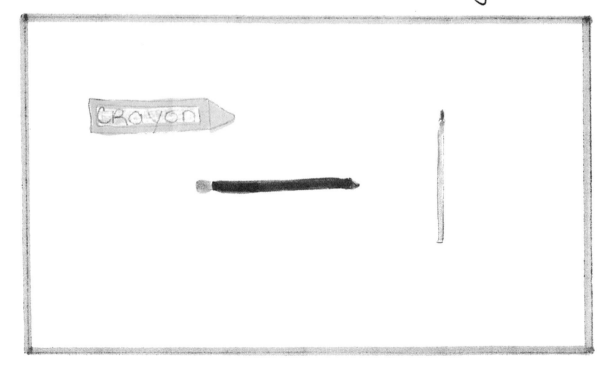

Which one can you catch in a net?

Which one can you drive?

Which one of the three twinkles?

Which one is dangerous?

Which ones can climb trees?

What picks you up to go to school?

Which animal can give

Milk?

Which animal can roar?

Which toy can you bang on?

Which one can sit in a tree?

Which one is the foot?

the pear?

Which one is the stop sign?

the cup?

Which One is the

Bee ?

Boat ?

Can you find

the hotdog?

the fish?

Can you find

the grapes?

the bananas?

Can you find

the carrot ?

Can you find the chicken?

"The Library"

What can you get at
the Library ?

Goat

Cow

Deer

Dolphin

Elephant

Lion

Ant

Mouse

Alligator

Turtle

Hippopotamus

Pony

Penguin

Pig

Rabbit

Snake

Duck

Butterfly

drum

car

house

heart

Sock

Shoes

Key

Hat

Fox

Frog

Kite

Top

ball

birthday cake

bicycle

cap

Which one is the

square ?

baseball ?

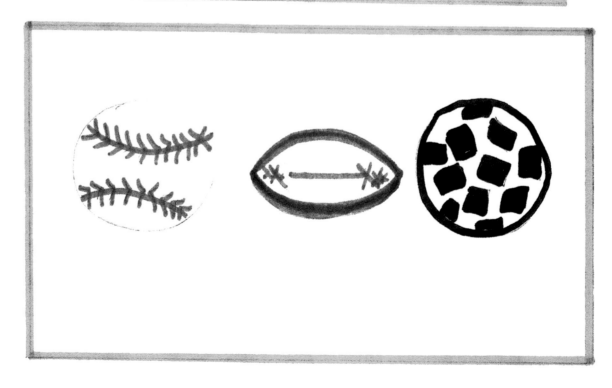

Which one is the SOCK ?

Pumpkin ?

Which One is the worm?

crayon?

Primary Colors

Secondary Colors

Colors and Shapes

Circle

Oval

triangle

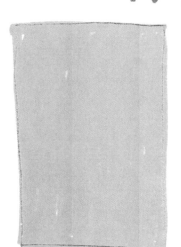

Rectangle

Square

CIOCK

What time is it?

CLOCK

What number is missing?

CIOCK

What number is missing?

Clock

What number is missing?

A a B b C c

D d E e F f

G g H h I i

J j K k L l

M N O
m n o
P Q R
p q r
S T U
s t u
V W X
v w x

Y y Z z

The alphabet in sign language.

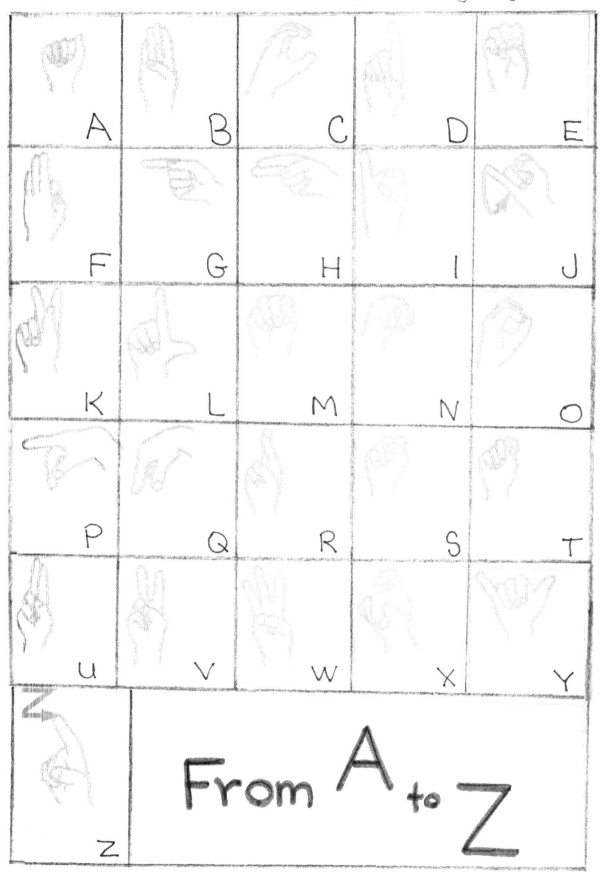

From A to Z

The 5 (five) Senses

Sight   eyes

hearing   ears

Smell   nose

taste   tongue

touch   fingers

How many balloons?

How many Squares?

How many circles?

How many stars?

How many hearts?

How many leaves?

How many notes ?

How many moons ?

How many dots ?

How many bows ?

How many balloons are blue ?

How many balloons are pink ?

How many balloons are Red?

How many balloons are Yellow?

77

How many balloons are purple ?

How many balloons are green ?

How many balloons are blue ?

How many balloons are pink ?

How many paint cans have the same paint color in each square?

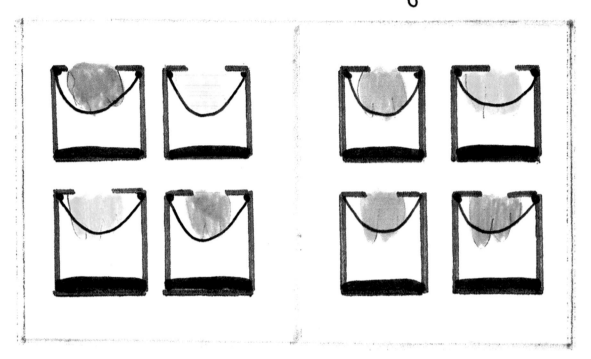

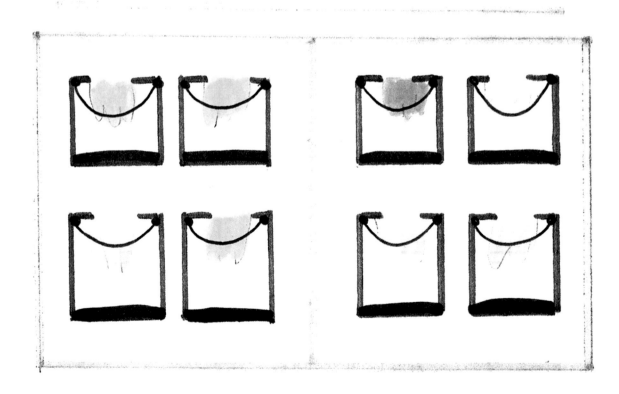

How many paint cans have the same
paint color in each square?

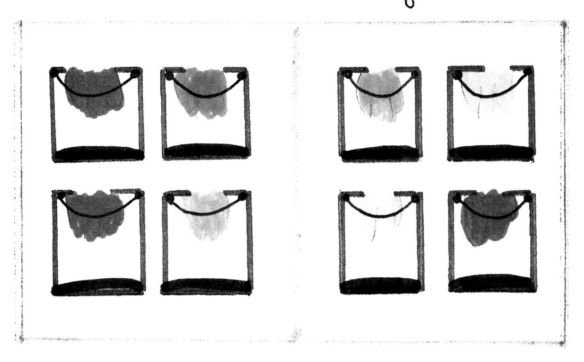

Who am I ?

Which one is the girl?

Which one is the boy?

Which one is the school teacher?

Which one is the librarian?

Who am I ?

Which one is the coach?

Which one is the mailman?

Which one is the Policeman?

Which one is the Astronaut?

What to put on first when you get dressed.

Girls

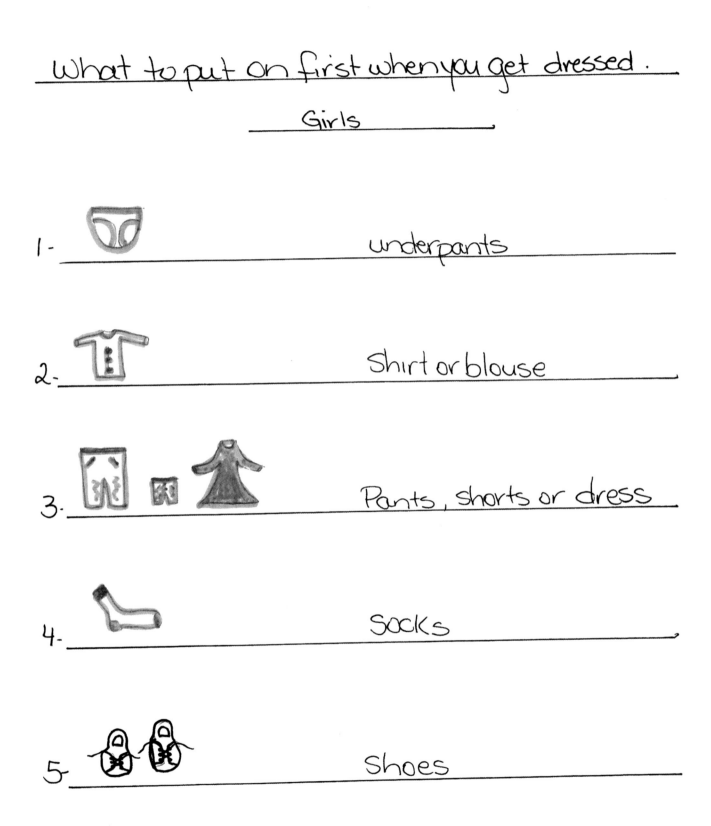

1- underpants

2- Shirt or blouse

3. Pants, shorts or dress

4- Socks

5 Shoes

What to put on first when you get dressed.
Boys

1 - underpants

2 - t shirt

3 - shirt

4 - pants or shorts

5 - sock's

6 - shoe's

Check Your Work checklist

Did I

○ Put my name on my paper?

○ Did I follow all directions?

○ Is my work neat?

○ Did I finish my work?

○ Are my words spelled correctly?

○ Did I do my best?

○ Did I put it where I can find it?

○

○

Things to Do
When school is out.

Read	Draw
Write	Study
Play	Help Out
Clean	Create
_____	_____

Wiggles and Giggles

• Where is your head?

• Where are your toes?

• Where are your ears?

• Where's your nose?

• Clap your hands?

• Nod your head yes

• Shake your head no

Stick out your tongue

Now tuck it back in

Open your mouth

Now close your mouth

Turn to the right

Now turn to the left

And now you are all done

Fun things you should know.

1. What do you use when it's raining?

    Umbrella or Frying Pan

2. What do you put on your head when it's cold outside?

    Hat or Shoes

3. What do you put on your feet when it's snowing outside?

    Boots or Boxes

4. What can you wear when it's warm outside?

    Shorts or Pants

5. What do you take off when you go into the pool?

    Socks and Shoes or A book

6. What do you brush before you go to bed?

    Hair or Your Teeth

7. What do you put on your hands when it's cold outside?

    Gloves or Slippers

8. What do Daddy and Mommy was the floor with?

    Box or Mop

9. What do horses eat?

    Hay or Cookies

10. Where do you pump air into on a bicycle?

    Seat or Tires

11. What animal has black stripes?

Zebra or Pig

12. What can you give Mommy for a present?

Flowers or Beach Ball

13. What do you put on when it's cold outside to keep warm?

Pajamas or A coat

14. What does Daddy and Mommy drive when they take you places?

Cars and Trucks or A Scooter

15. What do children wait for in the mornings to go to school?

School Bus or Horse

16. What do children pull behind them?

Wagon or Ball

17. What do Daddy and Mommy sweep the floor with?

Broom or Stick

18. What animals do kids want to bring home for pets?

Cats and Dogs or A Elephant

19. What do kids like to watch on television?

Cartoons or Movies

20. What do you use when you color in your coloring books?

Pens or Crayons

21. Who climbs down the chimney at Christmas time?

Easter Bunny or Santa Clause

22. What do most people eat on Thanksgiving Day?

Turkey or Bacon

23. What color is always used on Valentine's Day?

Blue or Red

24. What do you color for Easter?

Eggs or Cereal

25. Where do most people go on Easter Sunday morning?

Shopping or Church

26. When you are in class, who mostly writes on the chalkboard?

Teacher or Principal

27. What smells pretty?

Flowers or Bugs

28. What would be more fun taking a trip in?

Choo Choo Train or Bus

29. What would you rather take a ride on?

Horse or Cat

30. What would you help Daddy and Mommy do?

Take out the garbage or Pick up my toys

Printed in the United States
By Bookmasters